HIGHLIGHTS OF SCOTLAND

A Concise Traveler's Guide to Destinations & History

First Edition

By

RICHARD MCGEE

First Edition March 2024

Interior photos: Richard and Joyce McGee

ISBN 979-8-9901825-0-9 (paperback)
ISBN 979-8-9901825-1-6 (eBook)

Published by Glenstrae LLC
www.richard-mcgee.com

Table of Contents

MAP OF SCOTLAND

Figure 1: Map of Scotland[i]

INTRODUCTION

The sky was angry,
The peak of Ben Lomond was shrouded in mist,
This is where Rob Roy and my ancestors lived,
It was more than I imaged it to be.

Richard McGee

Scotland is a small country with an ancient history and breathtaking scenery. It is roughly the size of the state of South Carolina. It is not a populous country with only 5.5 million people, about the same as the state of Minnesota.

This book is a product of my research and travels to Scotland since 2019. The recommendations are my own. This book gives the reader a condensed view of travel to this beautiful country. You can use the book in a couple of ways: 1) as a companion to the comprehensive travel books from Rick Steves or Fodor's, or 2) as a tool to assist in planning your own trip.

There is a lot to see in Scotland. It is a challenge to decide where to go. The good news is you really can't go wrong. An Edinburgh taxi driver recently told me you can, "just drive to any village and you will find something interesting."

Scotland consists of three distinct regions: Highlands, Lowlands, and the Isles. The Highlands comprise the northern two-thirds of the country. The land is dominated by mountain ranges and deep glens. The Lowlands include the southern one-third of the country and the east coast. This land is more suited for agriculture. Scotland has about eight hundred islands, almost one hundred are populated. The islands are concentrated off the west and northern coasts.

Scotland is distinct from England. Both countries are members of the United Kingdom which is comprised of four countries: England, Scotland, Wales, and Northern Ireland. England and Scotland have a history of war and conflict. The country is split with about half of the population in favor of complete independence from England. A vote for independence was narrowly defeated in 2014.

The British monarchy reigns as the ceremonial head of state. Queen Elisabeth II was residing at her Scottish private estate, Balmoral, when she passed in 2022. Since she was in Scotland at the time of her death, she was taken to St. Giles Cathedral in Edinburgh to lie in state prior to her funeral in England.

The people of Scotland are friendly. It is a relatively safe country with good public transportation. The people are tolerant and helpful to visitors. I always recommend the traveler play it safe and use common sense in any country. Every nation has some crime. A little caution goes a long way.

The reason for my first trip to Scotland was to view the scenery. I was not disappointed. The Highlands are especially beautiful. There are more than 1,000 castles in Scotland. Scotland is a country of water. There are more than 31,000 freshwater lochs. Loch is the Gaelic word for lake or sea inlet.

Scotland is a great destination for those interested in history. My ancestors immigrated from Scotland and I have traveled to many sites of family importance. The first chapter of this book contains a condensed version of Scottish history. I have included chapters on Clan Campbell (The Campbells Are Coming) and Clan MacGregor (The Nameless Clan) for those with interest in those surnames.

Literary giants Robert Louis Stevenson, Robert Burns, and Sir Walter Scott, were Scots. Their writing was influenced by the culture and beauty of their homeland. Burns penned the lyrics to a song we sing on New Year's Eve: "Auld Lang Syne." Stevenson wrote the novels *Treasure Island* and *Strange Case of Dr. Jekyll and Mr. Hyde*. Sir Walter Scott, a lawyer by training, is known for the novels *Rob Roy* and *Ivanhoe*.

Scotland is a destination for whisky pilgrims. The country has about 140 distilleries, the greatest concentration of any country in the world. The oldest distillery was founded in 1775. The founders of the Maker's Mark brand of Kentucky bourbon trace their family history to Scotland.

Whatever your reason to visit Scotland, you can travel to fascinating sites to satisfy your interests. It is my desire to help you plan a wonderful trip that will have you to wanting to return.

Stirling Old Town

HISTORY OF SCOTLAND

There is much debate on the history of Scotland, especially ancient history and the origin of the native tribes and their languages. This is not a surprise since written accounts before the first century AD are virtually nonexistent. I have leaned upon commonly accepted history. The reader should understand that my account is reasonably accurate but may not be precise.

Archeologists have determined there were ancient civilizations in Scotland in the stone age. The stone remnants on the island of Jura may be the oldest structures in the country. Ancient sites exist in several locations across the country. Some of the best preserved are the village of Skara Brae on the island of Orkney. Skara Brae existed about 3,000 BC and can be visited by the traveler.

The Celts immigrated from Ireland around the fourth century BC. They created the clan system with each family group headed by a chieftain. The genesis of the Celts is murky, with some historians claiming origins in Egypt.

Recorded history begins with the arrival of the Romans in the first century. The Romans advanced into Scotland and were eventually driven southward by the Picts. The Romans called them Picts possibly because of the Latin word picti which means "painted." The Picts had the custom of painting their bodies. Not much is known of their origin. They could have been older relatives of the Celts.

The Romans built Hadrian's Wall to protect their northern border. What remains can be visited today. The wall runs for over seventy miles, east to west. Hadrian's Wall was built near the current border between Scotland and England. The land north of the wall was called Caledonia by the Romans. The Romans made several unsuccessful attempts to invade north of the wall. They eventually gave up and completely withdrew from Britain in the fifth century.

After the Romans, Scotland was populated by a mixture of Gaelic tribes from Ireland, called Scotti, and Picts. The Vikings entered into this mix when they began to invade in the eighth century. These groups found a tenuous level of coexistence and intermarried. The Picts and Scots were united under the rule of the House of Alpin near the beginning of the ninth century. Family members of the House of Alpin ruled until the 13th century.

The Scots allowed King Edward I of England to inject himself into a dispute over the Scottish throne in 1292. This was a mistake. He seized the throne of Scotland by force in 1296 and forced King John Baliol into exile. Edward removed the Stone of Destiny from Scotland and sent it to London. The stone on which Scottish kings were crowned would not return until the 20th century. The Wars of Scottish Independence were about to begin.

William Wallace (known as Braveheart to movie fans) united the Scots in a series of guerrilla attacks on the English. This reached a peak when Wallace and Andrew de Moray defeated a much larger English force at the Battle of Stirling Bridge on September 11, 1297. King Edward returned the following year and defeated Wallace at the Battle of Falkirk in an open field battle. The Scots returned to their strength of guerrilla warfare after this by skirmishing in northern England.

William Wallace was betrayed by John de Menteith in 1305. Wallace was taken to London, convicted in a sham trial, and executed. King Edward installed Englishmen and Scots who were loyal to the Crown to rule the country. England held power over most of the country again.

Robert the Bruce, who had previously sworn loyalty to Edward I, changed sides and began a campaign to organize the Scots to oppose the English. He was crowned King of Scotland on March 25, 1306. The English army moved north once again and defeated Bruce at the Battle of Methven that same year. He regrouped the following year and defeated the English at the Battle of Loudoun Hill.

King Edward I had enough of this. He personally took over the English army and moved north in 1307. Edward never made it to Scotland. He became ill during the trip and died on July 6, 1307. The English returned to London to bury their king. Bruce, meanwhile, fought several battles in

Scotland against clan groups loyal to the English Crown. A united Scotland was now opposed by King Edward II. The English king returned with a large force in 1314 and was defeated by Bruce at the Battle of Bannockburn.

The Scottish Crown remained with the descendants of Bruce until the Union of the Crowns in 1603. King James VI of Scotland ascended to the English throne as King James I of England upon the death of his childless cousin, Queen Elizabeth I. The crowns of Scotland and England have remained united to the present day. There has been much turmoil in the monarchy over the centuries. The transition between monarchs has not always been smooth. There was even a period where a bureaucrat, Oliver Cromwell, ruled in place of a monarch.

King James II was deposed in 1688 and went into exile in France. He had significant support in Scotland, especially in the Highlands. King James was Catholic like most in the Highlanders. A series of uprisings occurred in the 18th century in an effort to place James, and later his heir, back on the throne. The supporters of James were called Jacobites.

The third Jacobite uprising began in 1745 when Charles Edward Stuart, the grandson of James II, traveled from France to lead the rebellion in Scotland. The Jacobites had success at the beginning of the campaign however they were soundly defeated at the Battle of Culloden in 1746. The Jacobites were beaten by a far superior English force.

The battle was over quickly with over 1,200 Jacobite fatalities.

This was the last of the Jacobite uprisings, all of which were put down by the English. These uprisings were more than a fight for the Crown. They were also a form of civil war among the clans. Some Highland clans did not support the Jacobites and fought on the side of the Crown. The Battle of Culloden marked the end of the clan system in Scotland. Oppression would be unleashed in order to discourage further rebellion.

Atrocities occurred immediately after the battle. Injured Jacobite fighters who lay in the field at Culloden were either killed or stripped of their clothing and left to die. Jacobite sympathizers were hunted and killed in the weeks to follow. Highland dress, including the kilt, was banned. Highlanders were not allowed to carry weapons. The authority of clan chieftains was abolished and replaced by sheriffdoms who reported to the Crown. The Gaelic language spoken by the Highlanders had been banned in 1616, and was suppressed further after Culloden. Highland culture was extinguished.

A forced depopulation, known as the Highland Clearances, began in the middle of the 17th century and lasted for about a hundred years. Agriculture had always been marginal in the Highlands. There were few landowners in Scotland. That remains an issue today. The majority of the population were tenants or living on the land under hereditary custom. Small farms were consolidated into larger ones because they were more profitable. The presence of sheep was increased as they were more profitable than people.

Clan chiefs held no power over hereditary land claims after the Battle of Culloden. It is estimated that 70,000 people were forced to leave their homes. This caused significant immigration to other countries. The number of direct descendants in North America is greater than the population of Scotland today.

A rebirth of Highland culture occurred in 1822 when King George IV visited Scotland. Sir Walter Scott orchestrated the event. The king was fond of Scott's writing. The novel *Rob Roy* had been published in 1817. Even though Scott's novels were fantasized versions of historical events, they humanized the values of the Highlanders. The king wore Highland garb during his visit. This legitimized Highland dress and created modern kilt fashion as we know it today.

Scotland played a vital part in World War II. Prime Minister Winston Churchill ordered the creation of the British Commandos in 1940. Small groups of special forces were trained to make strikes behind enemy lines. Commandos were trained at Achnacarry in the Highlands.

Scapa Flow in the Orkney Islands became the primary naval base for the British fleet in World War II. It was selected because of its northerly location. Even so, it endured multiple attacks from the Germans during the war.

Modern Scotland has its own parliament for most matters. The parliament of Great Britain in London retains the right to determine what can be governed by the Scots. The Scottish Parliament was reconvened in Edinburgh in 1999 and moved into a modern building in 2004. The construction of the unique building was marred by delays and massive cost overruns. The architecture has its critics too.

Healthcare is nationalized in Scotland. The National Health System is the largest employer in the country. Taxes are higher in Scotland than the rest of the United Kingdom. Energy costs are high as well. Petrol prices are roughly double those of the United States. Energy independence has become a major issue. The United Kingdom is not able to provide half of its energy needs. Energy inflation has had a profound negative impact on the cost of living in recent years.

Traces of Scotland's past abound. Kilts are worn by many tour guides. Bagpipe buskers perform on city streets. Formal Highland dress is popular for weddings. The National Trust for Scotland and Historic Environment Scotland preserve and maintain many of the historic sites in the country. It is all waiting for the traveler to discover.

Statue of Robert the Bruce at Stirling Castle

TRAVEL SCOTLAND BASICS

Scotland is all about the destinations, scenery, and history. That is the primary focus of this book. I recommend making hotel accommodations through a reputable travel agent or web service. Guided tour vendors typically provide room and board on multi-day trips. It is important to plan ahead. Rural areas like the Highlands are sparsely populated and accommodations can be limited.

When To Travel

Scotland is beautiful year-round. It is most crowded in the summer months. The best time to enjoy decent weather and less crowding is in the shoulder season which is May through early-June, and mid-September through October. A tour guide told me that she enjoys the shoulder season because it is less stressful. Tour drivers must navigate their vehicles into destination parking areas and it can get hectic in the peak months.

Don't avoid Scotland if you must travel in peak season. There are some things you can do to make it a good experience. Make reservations well in advance. Arrive at destinations early in the day or in the evening to avoid crowds. This is an advantage for travelers who rent a car.

Scotland is farther north of the equator than the United States. That means the days are longer in the summer months and shorter in winter. Summer solstice in late June is the longest day of the year. Edinburgh enjoys 17 hours and 37 minutes of daylight on this day. The shortest day is winter solstice in late December. Edinburgh has only 6 hours 45 minutes of daylight on winter solstice. This is more pronounced farther north. An Inverness tour guide told me it gets dark at about 3:30 PM in the winter.

Scotland has a temperate maritime climate. It is an island country. The temperature is moderate because of the effect of the Atlantic Ocean and the North Sea. The average high temperature in summer is a pleasant 64 degrees Fahrenheit. The average high temperature in winter is a manageable 45 degrees Fahrenheit.

Scotland, like Ireland, is a green country because it rains a lot. Average annual rainfall is 78 inches. It is wetter in the western Highlands with rainfall of about 120 inches per year. The weather is unpredictable. You can experience several seasons in one day. This does not detract from the beauty of the country. The traveler who is prepared will enjoy Scotland in spite of the changing weather. I have experienced periods of rain, mist, wind, and sunshine during each of my trips. Travelers who are looking for a sunny getaway will probably not enjoy Scotland.

Ben Nevis is the tallest peak in Scotland and the United Kingdom. I've never seen the summit. It has been shrouded in mist each time I have visited the area. While disappointing, it does not detract from the beauty of the area. It enhances it in some ways.

Safety

The emergency number in the United Kingdom is 999 and 112. This is equivalent to 911 in the United States.

Scotland is relatively safe. I am not concerned about standing out like I would in other European countries. I try to blend in out of respect for locals. The Scots won't hassle you if you wear your NFL gear in their country. You will just stick out as an American.

Scotland has some crime, just like any country. Some common-sense techniques will make it safer. I recommend that wallets be carried in the front pocket. A cross-body bag is a safer option for purses. Small cross-body bags can be worn underneath a sweater or jacket.

Money

Currency in the countries of the United Kingdom is the pound Stirling (£). You can convert dollars to pounds in airports and post office locations in Scotland. The most convenient and economical method is to convert money at your local bank before travel. Our bank charges a fee of $10 to convert currency.

Credit cards are widely accepted in Scotland. Restaurants, stores, public transport, and taxis accept major cards. I travel with a Visa card and have never had it rejected. I use cash for small purchases. Coin denominations include £1 and £2 coins; these would compare to paper currency in the United States. The lowest denomination of paper currency in Scotland is the £5 note.

What To Pack

You should be able to pack everything you need for a one to two-week trip in a carry-on size suitcase and a backpack. Medication and personal essentials should be packed in your backpack. You want them with you if you get separated from your suitcase. Some airplanes have limited overhead space. Passengers who are among the last to board may be forced to check their carry-on case. Pack one change of clothes in your backpack if possible.

My packing list includes:

- Three-season jacket (with hood in the collar)
- Gloves, neck gaiter, & beanie – when traveling in any season other than summer
- Travel umbrella – mine fits inside a pouch in my backpack
- Electrical power adaptor – Type G
- Sunglasses
- Water resistant shoes

- Clothing that can be layered
- Earplugs – these come in handy on airplanes
- Granola bars or Biscoff cookies

Dress is casual. Scots dress like Americans with a couple of exceptions. It is rare to see a Scot wearing screen-printed apparel, however it is more common than a few years ago. The same is true for baseball-style caps.

Language

The most common language is Scottish English. It is basically the same as American English with some unique words. The Scots typically say "wee" as a replacement for "small." It is easy to understand a Scot, other than the occasional confusion with their accent. For example, Scots drop the "g" sound from most words. Edinburgh is pronounced "Ed-in-burrah." Scots is a dialect that differs from English in terms of vocabulary.

Scots Gaelic, pronounced "Gallic", was the common language in the Highlands. It was imported into Scotland by settlers from Ireland in the fifth and sixth centuries. The Education Act of 1872 made English the only language in schools. There are about fifty thousand residents who speak Gaelic as their native tongue today. This is confined to the western coast of the Highlands and the western islands.

Gaelic is undergoing a bit of a comeback as it is being taught in many schools. Gaelic words such as loch (lake) and glen (valley) have become ingrained in Scottish English. Road signs in Scotland include Gaelic and English place names. Inverness in Gaelic is "Inbhir Nis."

I have not had any major problems communicating in Scotland. Word pronunciation is an adventure from time to time. I once pronounced the name of the Scottish football team Celtic as "Keltic" and was corrected - twice. Scots, like most Europeans, take their football (soccer) seriously.

Road signs in Gaelic and English

Scottish Words

I have compiled a list of words you may hear while in Scotland. Travelers are not required to use them. Scots understand the American English version of words as well. I have learned that Scots generally appreciate attempts to use their language even if the pronunciation is butchered.

Aye = Yes
Loch = Lake or sea inlet
Hoachin' = Very Busy
Lift = Elevator
Lassie = Young girl
Laddie = Young boy
Bairn = Small child
Bonnie = Beautiful
Queue = Waiting Line
Ken = Know, or You know
Firth = A narrow arm of the sea

Ben = Mountain
Hiya = Hello
Glen = Valley
Wee = Small
Tatties = Potatoes
Bonnet = Hat
Lorrie = Truck
Crisps = Potato chips
Chips = French fries
Lift = Elevator

Classification of Mountains

Mountains can be found throughout Scotland. The majority are located in the Highlands and western islands. Hill walking is a popular pastime for locals and tourists. Few of the mountains require technical mountain climbing skills to reach their peak. The tallest mountains are called Munros. These are over 3,000 feet in elevation. Munro bagging is popular in Scotland. Climbers attempt to "bag" as many of the 282 Munros as they can.

The mountains of Scotland are classified by height as follows:

Munro: Over 3,000 feet
Corbett: Between 2,500 feet and 3,000 feet
Graham: Between 1,969 feet and 2,499 feet
Donald: Between 2,000 feet and 2,999 feet, and situated south of the Highland Boundary Fault
Marilyn: Under 2000 feet in height, with a prominence of at least 500 feet

Electricity

You will need an adaptor to charge cell phones and electrical devices. Electricity is supplied at 230 Volts in the United Kingdom compared to 120 Volts in the United States. A Type G adapter is needed in Scotland. You'll need a Type C adapter if you travel to other countries in Europe outside the United Kingdom.

How To Travel

Air
Scotland can be reached by air with commercial airports in Edinburgh, Glasgow, Inverness, and Aberdeen. The airports in Edinburgh and Glasgow are less than ten miles from the city centers. One-way taxi to the city center will cost about £30. Trams are available to the city center in Edinburgh.

There is a six-hour time difference between Scotland and my home in the Central Time Zone in the United States. International flights from the United States to the United Kingdom usually depart late in the evening and arrive the next morning. You are fortunate if you can sleep well on an airplane. I am lucky if I can get an hour to two of sleep on an international flight. Check-in time for most hotels is 3:00 PM. Stay up if you can. Catch two or three hours of sleep after you check in. Have a good evening meal and try to stay up until bedtime, say 10:00 PM in Scotland. Get a good night's sleep and you should be ready to go the next day. This routine has worked well for me.

Please be aware you may have to use your hotel key card to operate the lights in your room. Newer hotels usually have a key card holder where you must insert a room key in order for the lights to work. This is a tactic to conserve energy. Hotel elevators (lifts) tend to be smaller in the United Kingdom than North America.

Hotels in the United Kingdom will allow you to store your baggage if you arrive before check-in time. Most will allow you to catch a nap in the lobby if you can't make it to check in time. I once walked to Hyde Park in London and took an hour-long nap on a park bench. That was all I needed to make it to bedtime.

I recommend a light day after your arrival, especially if this is your first international trip or if you have trouble with jet lag. Do some sight-seeing in the area around your hotel. I like to stay in a hotel in the city center when travelling to Edinburgh. The Royal Mile and Edinburgh Castle is a short walk.

Rail

Scotland can be reached by rail from England. LNER provides high-speed rail service from Kings Cross Station in London to Edinburgh Waverly. I recommend this if you spend time in London on your trip to the United Kingdom. The trip is only four and a half hours and the train reaches speeds of 125 miles per hour. LNER provides service to several cities in Scotland, including Glasgow.

ScotRail is the national rail service within the country. Service is reliable in my experience. ScotRail is a good way to travel between cities or take day trips from Edinburgh or Glasgow. First class seating on ScotRail is not worth the extra expense in my opinion. The seats and storage are the same size as standard seating. I do recommend first class on LNER as the coaches are very nice. You can buy tickets online for both LNER and ScotRail.

Automobile

Travel by car is a great way to have flexibility to move about the country. Auto rentals are available at airports and in the cities. I have rented from Enterprise at the Edinburgh airport and had a good experience. They were very busy however they were very professional and processed us quickly.

The major difference in the United Kingdom is they drive on the left side of the road. I was apprehensive about this but it turned out well. It took a while to get accustomed to this. The roads are narrower than in the United States. Take your time. A cab driver recommended that I "wave and smile" if I cut someone off.

The steering wheel is located on the right side of the car. I recommend renting a car with an automatic transmission. If you get a manual transmission, you will have to shift with your left hand. A friend rented a car with a manual transmission and let's just say it was an adventure. A navigation system is a good choice as well. You can request one from the rental agency when you book your rental. The navigation system in my car was very helpful in navigating roundabouts.

Bring a road map of Scotland if you rent a car. This saved our most recent trip. The A81 road was closed west of Port of Menteith. The navigation system was unable to process an alternate route. I had purchased a Collins 2023 Road Map of Scotland and was able to determine an alternate route. The navigation system eventually figured out what I was trying to do about halfway through the detour.

The roads in Scotland are labeled with a letter and a number. The letter designates the type of road:

M: Motorways are divided four-line highways like an Interstate

A: Major two-lane roads
B: Minor two-lane and single-track

Sometimes it is hard to tell the difference between an A or B road.

A single-track road is a one-lane road with passing places. It is up to the drivers to figure out who pulls over into the passing place. The driver nearest the passing place usually pulls into it while flashing their lights to let the oncoming driver know to come ahead. Single-track roads are not listed on most road maps.

Bus

I have not used the bus system to travel between cities. Tour guides tell me it is reliable. It is a lower cost alternative to car rental. The drawback is it isn't as flexible. Edinburgh, Glasgow, and Inverness have hop-on hop-off bus tours of the city. This is a good way to get the feel of the city and decide which places you want to visit close up. I used the Edinburgh hop-on hop-off bus and recommend it. This is a good activity for the day after your travel day. Inverness is a compact city and I did not use the hop-on hop-off bus there.

You can buy a 24-hour ticket for the hop-on hop-off bus. Passengers can get off at any stop and reboard later. The Edinburgh buses operated by City Sightseeing run from 9:00 AM to 6:00 PM. Check their website to confirm tour times before you go. Edinburgh and Glasgow routes operate year-round. Inverness routes operate from early April through late October. They have audio guides in several languages. You can book tickets on their website: city-sightseeing.com.

Taxi
A good way to call a taxi in Scotland is from hotel lobbies. Front desk staff are accommodating and willing to assist. Some hotels have a taxi call button at the front desk that you can use with training. Airports and many train stations have a taxi stand. Taxi drivers are friendly and most are willing to give you suggestions on things to see. Taxis accept credit cards or cash. Most taxi drivers will pre-arrange a return trip to your hotel if you want that option.

Tour Companies
Guided tours are a great way to see popular destinations. You can book day trips and multi-day trips. You can book tours focused on a theme such as whisky or *Outlander,* for example. I recommend two sources of booking tours: Rabbie's and Viator.

There are several advantages to guided tours. The guides know the roads, they know the history of your destinations, and they will usually recommend places to eat. A good tour guide will give the perspective of a local. I recommend the traveler book with operators who use small buses or coaches. Many destinations in Scotland are small in footprint. A large bus group makes them feel more crowded.

Rabbie's was founded in 1993 and specializes in small group tours. Their coaches have capacity for sixteen passengers. These smaller coaches are sufficiently nimble to navigate Scotland's narrow roadways. Rabbie's is named after the famous Scottish poet, Robert Burns. They offer tours from Edinburgh, Glasgow, Inverness, and Aberdeen. Rabbie's vehicles are clean and the guides are professional in my experience. Their website is rabbies.com.

Viator is a marketing company owned by TripAdvisor, an international brand. They are not a tour operator. Viator sells tours run by other companies, including Rabbie's. Bus size varies for the tour companies that work with Viator. We recently took a tour from Inverness on a midi-size bus. The tour operator was Highland Express Tours. The guide was a local who was knowledgeable of the area. Capacity of the bus was about thirty people. The Viator website is viator.com.

All of my tour experiences in Scotland have been good. Tour guides are polite and knowledgeable. We did have a cancellation in 2023. We booked a Loch Ness tour through Viator. The tour operator, Happy Tours Scotland, cancelled the tour the day before it was scheduled. They informed us that both of their buses were out of service. We were on a ScotRail train when we were notified of the cancellation. ScotRail trains have WI-FI so I was able to go to Rabbie's website and schedule a Loch Ness day trip for the next day.

We were fortunate the Rabbie's tour was not fully booked. It was late September and there were only seven people on our sixteen-passenger bus!

All-inclusive tours are a good option for travelers who want a trip that is completely planned and coordinated for them. A group of my family members enjoyed an all-inclusive tour of Ireland with CIE tours. They offer tours throughout the United Kingdom, Italy, and Iceland. They advertise their small group experience with a maximum group size of twenty-six. Their website is cietours.com.

Food

Food options are similar to America. You can dine in expensive restaurants or on a shoestring budget. Scotland has fast food restaurants but they are not as abundant as in the United States. A full English breakfast is available in most hotels, charging about £18 each. A lower price option is to buy drinks and pastries at local convenience stores like Sainsbury's and Co-op. Many of these stores offer sandwiches and lighter fare for lunch or dinner.

Reservations are recommended for higher quality restaurants. There are many restaurants in Edinburgh and Glasgow but they are not abundant in some towns. The pandemic took a toll on some. We were in Inverness during a marathon weekend and all the restaurants were full. Thankfully, I had booked a reservation in advance. Most major hotel brands have a restaurant on site and you can usually get a table without a reservation. Scottish restaurants don't rush their customers. You may need to ask the wait staff to bring you the check.

Customary tipping is 10% to 15%. A service charge may be added to your bill to cover the tip. This may not be clear on the bill, so look carefully. Don't tip twice. The best way to tip is to leave cash for the wait staff, assuming there is no service charge.

Traditional Scottish food is available in many restaurants and pubs. Haggis is a pudding containing sheep organs. You will have to try it in Scotland if you want a taste. It is not legal in the United States because it contains sheep lungs.

Whisky is the drink that is most associated with Scotland. Those who don't drink alcohol can sample the other national drink, a popular carbonated soda, Irn-Bru, pronounced "Iron Brew." It has a unique taste that is hard to describe.

Neighborhood pubs aren't like bars as we know them in the United States. It is common to see adults with their children in pubs. Pubs are more like a communal gathering place. They can get loud and a bit wild on weekend nights in tourist areas. If you want to avoid the rowdier part of pub life, go earlier in the day.

DESTINATIONS

There is something for everybody in Scotland. The reader is encouraged to build their trip around those destinations that spark their interest. You can't go wrong. And you can always go back if you don't see everything on your first trip.

There are some destinations you'll want near the top of your list if you are a whisky pilgrim or a fan of entertainment franchises. I'll cover those in later chapters.

Travelers should be aware that historical sites in Scotland are old and may have accessibility limitations. These buildings were built centuries before accessibility regulations were in place. The United Kingdom does have accessibility laws which apply to modern buildings.

Edinburgh

The historical, cultural, and government capital is located on the east coast of Scotland on the banks of the Firth of Forth. Edinburgh is both an ancient and a modern city. The focal point of the city is Edinburgh Castle which sits above the town on a granite outcrop, Castle Rock. The cities of Edinburgh and Glasgow are on opposite sides of the country but are only an hour and a half apart by train. The Central Belt of Scotland is the most populous area of the country. It includes the two major cities and the area between them.

Edinburgh Castle

The medieval castle dominates the skyline from its perch above the city. Archaeological excavations indicate Castle Rock was occupied in the late Bronze Age or early Iron Age. The oldest stone building on the site is St. Margaret's Chapel. It was built in the 11th century by King David I and dedicated to his mother. Any other buildings at that time would have been built from wood.

Edinburgh Castle

Historians claim the castle was the most besieged in Europe. It has passed between English and Scottish control several times over the centuries. King Robert the Bruce ordered the castle be damaged in 1314 to prevent re-occupation by the English.

Royal apartments and a Great Hall were built in the 15th century. The castle served as a royal house until the construction of the more comfortable Holyrood Palace in the 16th century near the bottom of the Royal Mile. Mary Queen of Scots gave birth to the future king of Scotland and England, James VI and I, in Edinburgh Castle in 1567.

The castle became a military garrison after the Unification of the Crowns in 1603 and was used for military purposes through World War II. Historic Environment Scotland has been responsible for care of the castle since 1991. It is the most visited tourist attraction in the country.

Visitors can tour the National War Museum of Scotland and view the Honours of Scotland (the Scottish crown jewels) at Edinburgh Castle. The Stone of Scone upon which Scottish kings were crowned resides in the castle. The stone, also called the Stone of Destiny, continues to be used to crown the British monarch. It was transported to London for the coronation of King Charles III in 2023.

The castle has café food and drink available for purchase. This is nice because your visit may last several hours. After lunch, stay for the firing of the one o'clock cannon. This tradition began in 1861 to signal the time of day to ships in the harbor. It became popular with visitors and continues to the present. The cannon is fired every day except Sundays, Good Friday, and Christmas.

Military Tattoo

The Royal Edinburgh Military Tattoo occurs every year in August. The term "tattoo" describes that last call of duty of the day. The event features performances by military bands and civilian teams. The event is held on the esplanade to Edinburgh Castle. Temporary seating is erected to seat 8,800 guests for performances. I have not attended the Military Tattoo, but it is on my wish list.

Royal Mile

The cobblestone street that runs downhill from the castle to Holyrood Palace is the spine of the Old Town. The street changes names multiple times along the way: Castlehill, Lawnmarket, High, Canongate, and Abbey Strand. It is full of shops, restaurants, and churches. Stores have a range of products from fine Scottish wool items to kitschy souvenirs. The name of the street if fairly accurate; it is about a mile from top to bottom.

Palace of Holyroodhouse

The palace was built next to an abandoned 12th century abbey as a residence for the royal family. It was more comfortable than the drafty Edinburgh Castle. Holyrood Palace is an active royal residence. It is the official home of the British monarch in Scotland. It is closed to the public when royals are in residence.

King James IV converted the royal chambers on the site to a palace in the early 16th century. This was done about the time of his marriage to Margaret Tudor, sister of King

Henry VIII of England. The palace has been updated and enlarged over the centuries. Visitors can tour the apartment rooms of Mary Queen of Scots, the Great Gallery, and the Royal Dining Room.

Palace of Holyroodhouse

Scottish Parliament

The modernistic parliament building is located directly across the street from Holyrood Palace. The parliament body is often referred as Holyrood. The original Scottish Parliament was ended with the Acts of Union of 1707. It was re-established in 1999. The Scots have self-rule over most things excluding matters such as national defense. The current body is comprised of 129 Members of the Scottish Parliament who are elected to five-year terms.

Queen Elizabeth II opened the new Scottish Parliament building in 2004. Scots still get riled up over massive cost overruns for construction of the building. The thrifty Scots have a not-so-thrifty seat of government. The modern architecture of the building has its detractors as well. Visitors are welcome in the building for tours. If you make a visit to Holyrood Palace, it is worth a few minutes to walk across the street to see the parliament building.

St. Giles' Cathedral

King David I founded St. Giles' in 1124 as a Catholic Church. The current building is located about one-third of a mile east of Edinburgh Castle on the Royal Mile. The current structure was built in the 14th century and has been modified several times. The unique gothic spire resembles a crown.

Protestant reformer John Knox took over the church in 1559. St. Giles' became a Presbyterian church in 1560 when the Scottish Parliament abolished papal authority. It is widely believed that Knox is buried in the adjacent parking lot under spot number 23. St. Giles' still holds church services today. More than 20,000 mourners paid respects to Queen Elizabeth II after her coffin was conveyed to St. Giles' to lie in state in 2022. A memorial service was held in St. Giles' for the Queen on September 12, 2022.

Walking Tours

There are several one to three-hour guided walking tours available in Edinburgh. I've added this to the list because it was recommended by a taxi driver on my last trip. Walking tours include Edinburgh Castle, Edinburgh Underground, Harry Potter, Royal Mile, and a murder mystery. The Viator website has a comprehensive listing of Edinburgh walking tours.

HMY Britannia

Queen Elizabeth II launched HMY Britannia in 1953. The ship served as a royal residence for over forty years. It sailed the royal family all over the globe on hundreds of state visits. It was decommissioned in 1997 due to the cost to refurbish. John Major's government declined to spend £17 million for repairs.

All clocks on the Britannia remain stopped at 3:01 PM, the exact time the Queen left the ship for the last time. Britannia is located a mile and a quarter northeast of central Edinburgh in Leith harbor. Visitors can get there by taxi or tram.

Linlithgow

The birthplace of Mary Queen of Scots and King James V is located twenty miles west of Edinburgh in the Central Belt. Linlithgow Palace was a residence of the Scottish monarchy in the 15th and 16th centuries. The palace was little used after the Union of the Crowns. It fell into disrepair and was gutted by fire in 1746. It remains an impressive ruin.

Entrance to Linlithgow Palace and spire of St. Michael's Church

St. Michael's Church is adjacent to the palace. Built in the 15th century its original spire was of gothic design similar to St. Giles' Cathedral. The spire was damaged in 1768 and removed in 1821. A controversial aluminum spire was added in 1964.

Linlithgow is an easy day trip from Edinburgh. Visitors can travel on ScotRail from Edinburgh Waverly. The palace is a short walk from the rail station. You can walk the palace grounds down to the banks of Linlithgow Loch. Travelers should be aware parts or all of the palace may be closed for safety reasons. The palace is a ruin and under control of Historic Environment Scotland. Access was extremely limited when I was there however it did not detract from my visit. The Historic Environment Scotland website lists updates on site access.

Stirling Area

The strategic city of Stirling is located about halfway between Edinburgh and Glasgow at the north end of the Central Belt. Stirling sits on the southern border of the Highlands. Several crucial battles were fought here during the Wars of Scottish Independence. The Battle of Stirling Bridge and the Battle of Bannockburn were key points in the wars between the Scots and England. The main attraction is Stirling Castle.

Stirling is about forty miles northwest of Edinburgh. It is a great day trip from Glasgow or Edinburgh. Travel by automobile can be accomplished in less than an hour. Rail travelers can get to Stirling on a forty-five-minute trip from Edinburgh Waverly via ScotRail. The train station is less than a mile from Stirling Castle. I recommend rail travelers take a taxi to the castle and return on foot. Your walk back to the station is downhill. The parking lot at the castle can get full in high season. Castle visitors who arrive by car may have to park in town.

Stirling Castle

The two most important castles in Scotland are Edinburgh Castle and Stirling Castle. Both were occupied by Scottish monarchs during their history. Most of the present buildings at Stirling Castle were built by the later Stuart monarchs in the 15th and 16th centuries. Stirling Castle, like Edinburgh Castle, sits atop a volcanic outcrop and dominates the local skyline. Steep cliffs around the castle enhance the defensive nature of the site.

Stirling Castle

The Royal Palace at Stirling Castle is furnished to resemble its appearance when King James V was monarch. The Great Hall was completed in the early 16th century during the time of King James IV. It was built as a showplace for the monarchy and hosted banquets and dances. The Chapel Royal was built by King James VI for the baptism of his son. It is the last building constructed at the castle.

Mary Queen of Scots was crowned at Stirling Castle in 1542. Her son, King James VI and I was crowned near the castle in the Church of the Holy Rude in 1567. It is the only remaining active church in Scotland to host a coronation. The church is a short walk downhill from the castle. Check the church website holyrude.org for hours of operation.

Battle of Stirling Bridge
The Stirling Old Bridge is located on the site where William Wallace defeated the English at the Battle of Stirling Bridge in 1297. The site is two-thirds of a mile north of the train station. The old bridge was built after the Battle of Stirling Bridge sometime in the 15th or 16th century. The battle was fought a half mile northeast of Stirling Castle. The English who occupied the castle at the time would have observed the battle from the ramparts.

National Wallace Monument: The tower monument to William Wallace is located one mile northeast of the Stirling Old Bridge. It is about two hundred feet tall.

Stationed atop Abbey Craig the visitor can see Stirling and the Old Bridge from the top of the tower.

The Wallace Sword is located at the monument. Much debate has centered on the authenticity of the sword. Some historians believe the sword may contain pieces of the original Wallace sword. James IV ordered the sword be repaired to its current state.

Battle of Bannockburn Visitor Center
The decisive battle in the First War of Scottish Independence was fought a short distance south of the castle. Robert the Bruce defeated a much larger English army in 1314 by trapping them in marshy ground. The English horses sunk in the mud and became useless. Tickets are available for timed entry at nts.org.uk/visit/places/bannockburn.

Castle Campbell
Fifteenth century Castle Campbell was the Lowland home of the large Argyll Campbell clan. This unique castle is fourteen miles east of Stirling near the village of Dollar. The best way to get to the castle is by automobile. The access road to the castle from Dollar is extremely narrow. Large tour buses can't make the trip.

The tower of Castle Campbell is very well preserved. The remainder of the structure is in various stages of decay. Castle Campbell was burned in 1654 after the Anglo-Scottish War. The visitor who climbs to the top of the tower is rewarded with commanding views of Dollar and the valley below.

Doune

The small village of Doune is eight miles northwest of Stirling. The main attraction is Doune Castle. It was rebuilt to its present layout in the 14th century by the Duke of Albany, Robert Stewart, son of King Robert II. The castle is famous for its role in entertainment franchises such as *Outlander* and *Game of Thrones*.

Doune Castle gets extremely busy during high season. I know of one tour company that avoids it due to the crowds. Some companies with themed tours make stops at Doune. Travelers who arrive by automobile should arrive early or late in the day for less crowding. There is a small car park next to the castle. Visit the Historic Environment Scotland website for updates on operating hours. Tickets to the castle can be booked online.

The second destination at Doune is the Deanston Distillery just south of the city limits. The large building was a cotton mill that once employed 1,500 people. It shut down in 1965 and was transformed into a distillery the next year. The distillery sits on the banks of the river Teith. Water from the river is used for making whisky and to generate electricity. It is recommended to book tours in advance at deanstonmalt.com.

Doune Castle

Falkirk

The two primary attractions at Falkirk are the Kelpies and the Falkirk Wheel. Falkirk is a town of about thirty thousand people located fifteen miles southeast of Stirling. Falkirk was an industrial town that hit hard times. The Kelpies are two massive one-hundred-feet high horse heads. Kelpies are shape-shifting water spirits. They were built next to the M9 motorway to help attract tourists. Many guided tours going to the Highlands stop to view the Kelpies.

The Falkirk Wheel is an engineering feat. It is a rotary boat lift that transports boats from the Forth and Clyde Canal to the Union Canal. The Falkirk Wheel lifts boats a distance of seventy-nine feet. The Falkirk Wheel was part of a project to restore the two canals which had fallen into disrepair. It replaces multiple locks that were shut down in 1933. Queen Elizabeth II opened the Falkirk Wheel on May 24, 2002.

The Kelpies

The Highlands

> *My heart's in the Highlands, my heart is not here,*
> *My heart's in the Highlands, a-chasing the deer;*
> *Chasing the wild deer, and following the roe,*
> *My heart's in the Highlands, wherever I go.*[ii]
> *Robert Burns*

The rugged Highlands occupy the northwest portion of Scotland. The land was dominated by Gaelic-speaking clans until the 18th century. Clans fought among themselves for territory. The Romans were never able to conquer the Highlands. The English finally brought the clans to heel with their victory at Culloden in 1746.

The Highland Boundary Fault forms the southern geologic border of the Highlands. The fault crosses the country from Arran to Stonehaven. The relatively flat and rolling terrain of the Lowlands lie to the south of the fault. The Highlands are bisected by the Great Glen Fault which runs northwest from Fort William to Inverness. The fault runs directly underneath four lochs: Loch Ness, Loch Oich, Loch Lochy, and Loch Linnhe.

Glencoe

The steep-sided Glencoe valley is considered by many as the most beautiful spot in Scotland. Numerous guided tours include Glencoe on their itinerary. Glencoe is also popular with hikers and climbers. Often referred as "the weeping glen," it is the site of the 1692 Massacre of

Glencoe. Thirty-eight members of Clan MacDonald of Glencoe were murdered by a contingent of soldiers led by Robert Campbell of Glenlyon, acting on behalf of King William III.

Glencoe

Loch Lomond

Carved by glaciers during the last ice age, Loch Lomond is the largest loch on the island of Great Britain. It was home to Clan Buchanan, Clan MacGregor, and Clan Colquhoun. There are several islands on Loch Lomond. The largest, Inchmurrin, was the site of a 17th-century monastery. Access to Inchmurrin is by ferry. Visit inchmurrin-lochlomond.com for more information.

The east shore of Loch Lomond is dominated by Ben Lomond. It rises to an elevation of 3,196 feet and is the southernmost of the Munros (a mountain that exceeds 3,000 feet in elevation). All forms of water sports are popular on Loch Lomond. This is due to the size of the loch and its proximity to Glasgow. The southern shore is fourteen miles from the center of the city.

Several tour companies offer boat tours of Loch Lomond including Sweeney's Cruise Company, Loch Lomond Leisure Scotland, and Cruise Loch Lomond. The steam-powered paddle-wheeler Maid of the Loch was built in Glasgow and began operating in 1953. She fell into a state of disrepair and is being renovated by a nonprofit organization. The Maid can be visited at the Balloch pier.

Glenfinnan

Prince Charles Edward Stuart landed at Glenfinnan in 1745 from France to start the last of the Jacobite uprisings. A sixty-foot-high monument stands today in Glenfinnan to commemorate the event.   Stuart was the grandson of the exiled monarch James VII and II.

The Glenfinnan train viaduct was completed in 1898. It features twenty-one arches and rises one hundred feet above the hamlet. The viaduct is featured in several Harry Potter films along with the Hogwarts Express. The viaduct is the longest rail bridge in Scotland at 1,246 feet long.

Glenfinnan Viaduct

Visitors flock to Glenfinnan to see the train cross the viaduct. Arrive early to get a parking spot. If the lot is full, there is usually a place to park just up the hill at Saint Mary & Saint Finnan Church. The church is worth a visit due to the beautiful setting.

Jacobite Steam Train

The forty-two-mile route between Fort William and Mallaig is operated by West Coast Railways. The Jacobite crosses the Glenfinnan Viaduct on each run. Reservations can be made with the rail company at westcoastrailways.co.uk/jacobite/steam-train-trip   or through a tour company.

The locomotive of The Jacobite is an LMS Class 5MT, also known as The Black 5. These locomotives were built between 1934 and 1951. They are powered by coal-fired steam. West Coast Railways may use a diesel-powered locomotive during periods of high fire danger in the Highlands. The coaches on the train are from British Railways and were built in the 1960's.

The Jacobite is also known as the Hogwarts Express. The rail company provided the train and allowed filming of the rail line for the Harry Potter movies. The actual locomotive used in the movies is owned by the studio and kept in London. The steam locomotives used on the rail line are the same design. The Jacobite is recommended for travelers who like trains or are Harry Potter fans. The scenery along the route is first rate. A one-way run takes about two hours.

Readers should be aware that train service of the Jacobite was suspended for a time in 2023 due to safety concerns with the passenger car doors and windows. West Coast Railways and the Office of Rail and Road have been working on this issue. It is recommended that travelers who book trips on the Jacobite check the status of train operations before they travel.

Mallaig is a fishing village on the shore of the Atlantic Ocean. Ferries provide access to several western islands from Mallaig. The islands of Skye, Rum, and Eigg can be seen from Mallaig on a clear day. The village has lodging, food, and shops to accommodate tourists. The seafood is fresh and tasty.

Fort William

Fort William is the second largest town in the Highlands. The earliest fort was built here in 1654 to control the Highland population. Very little remains of the forts that were built here. The proximity of Fort William to multiple Highland tourist destinations has made it a popular location for lodging.

Ben Nevis dominates the eastern horizon of Fort William. The tallest mountain in the United Kingdom rises to 4,413 feet. The summit is about four and a half miles from town. This makes Fort William popular as a base for hikers and mountain walkers. Over 100,000 people climb Ben Nevis each year. Henry Alexander ascended the mountain in 1911 driving a Ford Model T.

Inverary

The ancestral seat of the Duke of Argyll is a small village of about 600 inhabitants. Inverary is on the western shore of Loch Fyne, the longest sea loch in Scotland. It is about sixty miles northwest of Glasgow. The main attraction is Inverary Castle, built in the 18th century by Archibald Campbell, the third Duke of Argyll. The prior castle was demolished to build the existing structure that is more mansion than castle. The village was demolished in the 1770s and moved a short distance to give the castle more space.

James V of Scotland visited the old castle in 1533. Queen Victoria visited Inverary in 1874. Her sixth child, Princess Louise, had married John Campbell in 1871. He was heir to the 8th Duke of Argyll and would become the 9th Duke in 1900.

Inverary Castle

Inverary Castle remains under the ownership of the Campbells; the 13th Duke of Argyll and his family live in private apartments within the structure. The interior features a large sixty-foot-high atrium known as the Armoury Hall. It holds a large collection of weaponry dating back to the 16th century.

Inverary Castle was featured in the 2012 Christmas episode of *Downton Abbey* as the fictional Duneagle

Castle. Rick Steves has also filmed on the grounds. The castle is open for visitors during tourist season. A café and gift shop are located on the basement level. Visit the castle website inverary-castle.com for tickets and more information. Tickets can be purchased at the castle as well.

Inverness

The largest city in the Highlands is home to 46,000 people. Inverness is located on the banks of the river Ness where it empties into the North Sea via the Moray Firth. Visitors can reach Inverness by air and train. ScotRail provides service from Glasgow and Edinburgh. The trip is three and a half hours from each city.

Inverness Castle sits on a hill above the eastern bank of the river. The castles that have stood on the site functioned primarily as a military garrison. The first castle was destroyed by Robert the Bruce in 1307 as part of his strategy to eliminate opposition to his crown. The current red sandstone structure is undergoing renovation and is scheduled to reopen in 2025.

Inverness is a good location for travelers to use as a base for exploring the northern Highlands. Tour companies provide day trips from Inverness to Loch Ness, Dunrobin Castle, Cawdor Castle, Culloden Battlefield, and the Isle of Skye. There is a distinct advantage for booking a Loch Ness day trip that originates in Inverness. The loch is a few minutes from town. A Loch Ness tour that originates in

Edinburgh will take about three hours just to reach the area.

There are several good hotels and restaurants in Inverness. And there is lots of live music. Restaurants can get crowded during weekends, especially when there is a special event. We made a reservation at the MacGregor's Bar restaurant and had an excellent meal. MacGregor's has live local music on a regular basis. Their music calendar can be found at macgregorsbars.com/whats-on.

Culloden Moor
The last battle to be fought on British soil happened here on 16 April 1746. Culloden is located a few miles east of Inverness. The National Trust for Scotland maintains the battleground where the last Jacobite uprising ended. The Culloden Visitor Center is tastefully done and sits to the side of the battlefield. Visitors have access to panoramic views of the battlefield from the roof. A museum contains artifacts from both sides of the battle. A café and gift shop are located in the visitor center.

Loch Ness
The most famous of all Scottish lochs is allegedly the home of the Loch Ness Monster. It is the largest loch in Great Britain by volume due to its great depth. With a maximum depth of 755 feet, Loch Ness does not freeze in the winter. Cold water on the surface falls and is replaced by warmer water from the depths.

Loch Ness is twenty-three miles long with Inverness at the northern end. The main source of water is River Oich which flows in at Fort Augustus at the southern end. The water in Loch Ness is dark and murky. The soil surrounding the loch is high in peat (partially decayed organic matter). Water runoff from the hills around the loch is stained by peat and is slightly acidic. The mystery of monsters is enhanced by the dark water.

There have been multiple reports of encounters with the Loch Ness Monster, or Nessie. The first was in the sixth century when St. Columba is said to have encountered a creature and ordered it to go back from whence it came. The famous 1934 photo of the monster is believed to be a hoax. Nessie is generally described as a reptilian creature with a long, thin neck. Numerous attempts to find credible existence of Nessie have failed.

Travelers can search for Nessie themselves. Tour boat excursions are available year-round from several vendors. We took a one-hour Loch Ness by Jacobite cruise from Clansman Harbour. It included a close-up view of Urquhart Castle. Their website is jacobite.co.uk. The top deck has open-air seating while the bottom deck is enclosed. Video screens display a depth scan so the tourist can observe any unusual objects below the surface.

The author looking for Nessie

The Falls of Foyers are a popular stopping point along the south shore of Loch Ness. The falls can be reached by a trail leading downhill from the car park. The path is steep but worth the walk. The Gaelic name for the falls is interpreted as the "smoky falls." Visitors can see why when they observe the dark peat-stained water flowing over the falls. The falls are not as impressive as they once were. Some of the water is being diverted to produce hydroelectric power.

The historic Invermoriston Bridge is five miles north of Fort Augustus along the north shore of Loch Ness. It was built by engineer Thomas Telford and opened in 1813. The center support makes use of an outcrop in the river. The bridge was replaced by a "new" bridge in 1933. A series of rapids, called the Invermoriston Falls, run under the bridges. The old bridge is no longer in use, but can be visited in the village of Invermoriston on the A82 road.

Urquhart Castle

The ruin of Urquhart is one of the most visited castles in Scotland. There are more impressive castles in Scotland, however the setting on the shore of Loch Ness makes Urquhart a place to visit. There is archeological evidence that suggests a fort existed at Urquhart as early as the sixth century. The current ruin was constructed in the 13th century.

Urquhart Castle

King Edward I of England captured Urquhart Castle in 1296 and again in 1303. He granted the castle to Clan Comyn because of their opposition to Robert the Bruce as king of Scotland. The Bruce captured the castle in 1307 about the same time he captured Inverness Castle.

Control of Urquhart Castle was contested during the next two hundred years between the Scottish crown and the powerful Clan MacDonald. King James IV gave Urquhart to the Grant clan in 1509. A struggle between the Grants and the MacDonalds would last another hundred years.

The English would gain control of Urquhart around the time of the first Jacobite uprising. They destroyed most of the castle in 1690 to prevent the Jacobites from using it. The castle is maintained by Historic Environment Scotland and remains as it was when it was destroyed.

Caledonian Canal

Stretching for sixty miles from Fort William to Inverness, the Caledonian Canal allowed ships to cross Scotland to avoid the dangerous Pentland Firth along the north coast. The canal follows the Great Glen Fault traversing through four natural lochs: Lochy, Oich, Ness, and Dochfour. Construction took place from 1803 to 1822.

Caledonian Canal lock at Fort Augustus

Manual labor was used to dig the canals since modern earth moving equipment had not been invented. About one-third of the canal was dug by hand while the rest of the canal made use of the natural lochs. Twenty-nine locks were built to allow ships to travel the canal system. The highest elevation of the canal is 106 feet above sea level. Queen Victoria took a trip along the canal in 1873.

Commercial ships are bigger nowadays and are unable to use the canal. The canal is still used for leisure and some commerce. The Scots consider the canal a major engineering feat. A restoration of the canal took place from 1995 to 2005 to upgrade and repair the lock system.

Loch Katrine

The primary source of water for Glasgow, Loch Katrine is located thirty miles north of the city. Queen Victoria opened the new aqueduct system on the 14th of October, 1859. Water flows by the force of gravity through two aqueducts into the Glasgow water system. The Loch Katrine aqueduct system was considered a major engineering feat in its day, and has been in use for 164 years.

Loch Katrine is eight miles long and approximately one mile wide. Rob Roy MacGregor was born near the west end of the loch. The area between Loch Katrine and Loch Lomond was home to the largest band of MacGregors in the early 18th century. The loch is a popular day trip due to its proximity to Glasgow. There are two access points: Trossachs Pier on the east end of the loch, and Stronachlachar on the west. The road to Stronachlachar is paved, with the last eleven miles being single track.

Boat cruises are available at Loch Katrine. One option is the steamship Sir Walter Scott which is based at Trossachs Pier. It was commissioned in 1900 and has recently been refurbished. The steamship is named after the famous Scottish writer who wrote the poem "The Lady of the Lake" which is based on Loch Katrine. Visit lochkatrine.com for more information about boat cruises.

Eilean Donan Castle

Located at the convergence of three sea lochs, Eilean Donan is one of the most beautiful castle sites in Scotland. The castle sits on an island and is connected to the mainland with a bridge. The original castle was built in the 13th century and was home to Clan MacKenzie. This castle was destroyed in 1719 to prevent the English from using it during the Jacobite uprisings.

Eilean Donan Castle

The current castle looks much older than its age of one hundred years. Eilean Donan castle was rebuilt in the early 20th century by John MacRae-Gilstrap. The bridge was added at this time to improve access to the grounds.

Eilean Donan is under private ownership and is a popular location for weddings. The castle is open for tours from February through December. I recommend a stop here, especially if you are visiting the Isle of Skye. Eilean Donan is eight miles east of the Skye Bridge. Visit eileandonancastle.com for more information.

The picturesque location of Eilean Donan has attracted the attention of the entertainment industry. Over thirty movies have been filmed here including the original *Highlander* starring Sean Connery, a Scotsman.

Oban

The village of Oban is located on the west coast of Scotland. The word Oban means "Little Bay" in Scots Gaelic. The natural harbor is protected by the island of Kerrera. Oban is a gateway to the western islands. Ferries provide regular service to Lismore, Colonsay, Islay, Coll, Tiree, Mull, Barra, and South Uist. Travelers can reach Oban by auto or rail from Glasgow.

Oban was built around the distillery which was founded in 1794. The Oban distillery was constructed from local granite and is located along the waterfront. The most prominent landmark in Oban is McCaig's Tower, started in 1895. John Stewart McCaig, a wealthy businessman, wanted to build the tower as a family monument. He hired local stonemasons to give them work during slow times. Construction was halted when McCaig died in 1902, and never resumed.

McCaig's Tower overlooking the Oban distillery and waterfront

Oban is a scenic village and is a regular stop for guided tours. There are some very good fish and chip restaurants in Oban. The fish is fresh from the ocean. Oban calls itself the "seafood capital of Scotland." A walk along the waterfront is a great way to catch views of the bay and visit local shops.

Ben Cruachan Power Station

Rising to an elevation of 3,694 feet above Loch Awe, Ben Cruachan is popular with hillwalkers. It is also called The Hollow Mountain because it holds a secret. Buried inside the mountain is a 440-megawatt pumped storage hydroelectric power station. Four turbines are housed in the main cavern.

Construction of the power station took about six years. The access tunnel to the main cavern is one kilometer in length. Cruachan Power Station was dedicated on October 15, 1965 by Queen Elizabeth II. Tours of the power station are available. You can arrange a tour through the station website. Check for availability at visitcruachan.co.uk. A visitor center is located on the site; it contains a café and gift shop. Exhibits are free. The visitor center is twenty miles west of Oban on the A85 road.

Islands

The islands fall into four groups: Inner Hebrides, Outer Hebrides, Orkney, and Shetland. The Hebridean islands reside off the western coast of Scotland. The Orkney and Shetland archipelagos are north of the mainland. Fishing is a major occupation of the islands. The islands that are populated do not have many residents. It is easy to see why. The unpredictable seas made it difficult for settlers to travel and receive supplies.

<u>Orkney</u>
The Orkney archipelago is ten miles off the northeast mainland and contains about seventy islands. The land is fertile and mostly devoid of trees. The population of Orkney is 21,000, down from a peak of 32,000 in the 1860s.

Orkney is famous for its prehistoric sites. The oldest known settlement is at Knap of Howar. Carbon-dating indicates the site to have been occupied in 3700 BC. It may be the oldest site in Great Britain. The Standing Stones of Stenness is a henge site that is older than Stonehenge and the Great Pyramids. Another stone circle, the Ring of Brodgar is within a mile of the Standing Stones of Stenness. The village of Skara Brae dates to about 3000 BC and contains the remains of ten stone houses.

Guided tours are available for travelers who want to see the prehistoric sites of Orkney. Travelers should be aware the weather can be unpredictable. Strong sea currents can cause the ferry services to suspend service. This is outside of the control of the tour companies. Travelers who plan trips to Orkney should have a backup plan in case of bad weather.

The Picts had settled in Orkney in the late Iron Age. Orkney and Shetland were settled by Vikings beginning in the eighth century. The islands remained under Norse rule until 1468 when they were transferred to Scotland as part of a dowry settlement.

Shetland

You can't go any farther north in the United Kingdom than the Shetland archipelago. Shetland is 110 miles north of the Scottish mainland and 140 miles west of Norway. Only sixteen of the one hundred islands are populated. The population of Shetland is 22,000, about the same as Orkney.

Shetland has many prehistoric and Iron Age sites. It was occupied by the Picts, and later by the Vikings. Like Orkney, Shetland was transferred to Scotland in 1468.

Shetland is a regular stop for cruise ships. Ships dock at Lerwick, the largest settlement in Shetland. Lerwick Harbor is protected by the island of Bressay which lies to the east.

Atlantic puffins reside in Shetland and Orkney from April to August. These colorful seabirds live in large colonies. They feed on fish by diving into the water. Shetland ponies, residents of the area for 4,000 years, can be seen grazing in the countryside.

Shetland enjoys extremely long days during the summer because of its northerly location. A summer day can be nineteen hours long near solstice, and it doesn't get completely dark during the night. This time of year is known as Summer Dim. Conversely, the shortest day is about five and a half hours of daylight at winter solstice.

Inner Hebrides

Thirty-five of the seventy-nine islands of the Inner Hebrides archipelago are inhabited. This island chain is located near the west coast of Scotland. The largest islands are Skye, Islay, and Mull. Total population of the Inner Hebrides is about 20,000. The Inner Hebrides are home to Clan MacLeod, MacDonald, MacLean, MacRory, Donald, MacKinnon, and MacDougall. Twenty percent of the population speak Gaelic.

The oldest prehistoric site in Scotland is on the island of Jura. Stone hearths found on Jura have been dated to 6000 BC. There is significant evidence of permanent settlements in the Hebrides in the Middle Stone Age.

The islands were occupied by the Picts and Gaels prior to the arrival of the Vikings in the eighth century. Island rule was contested between Irish and Norwegian groups beginning in the 12ᵗʰ century. Norwegian rule ended in 1266 with the Treaty of Perth.

The island clans operated as an independent society from the 12ᵗʰ through 15ᵗʰ centuries. Somerled, who was of mixed Norse-Gaelic ancestry, is widely considered the first of the ruling island clan chiefs. Their remote location isolated them from Scotland, Ireland, and Norway. They were capable seafarers who developed the birlinn, a vessel powered by oar and sail.

Skye

The Isle of Skye is the northernmost and largest island of the Inner Hebrides. With a population of 10,000, it is the most populous as well. Skye is one of the most visited places in Scotland because of its natural beauty and ease of access. Visitors can select from numerous guided tour options. The island is connected to the mainland with a bridge at Kyle of Lochalsh. Ferries also provide access to the island. The only operating turntable ferry in the world is located at Kylerhea.

The Scottish Clearances and collapse of the kelp industry had a major impact on Skye. The population of Skye today is less than half of what it was in the 19ᵗʰ century. Almost a third of the population speak Gaelic. The Scottish Gaelic college, Sabhal Mór Ostaig, is located on the Sleat peninsula.

Tourism is a major industry on Skye. The population swells in the summer months with tourists. The scenic beauty of the island has made it a must-see for travelers. Portree is the largest village on the island. It has a picturesque harbor and is a good place for travelers to use as a base to explore Skye.

Portree

The Cuillin Hills are dramatic bare mountains of igneous rock. They are the highest mountains in the Inner Hebrides and the most challenging to climb in Scotland. There are twelve Munros in the Cuillins. The Quiraing escarpment in north Skye is a massive slip-fault of pinnacled hills. The name Quiraing, comes from the Norse words kvi and rand, which means "round fold." The translation to Gaelic is Cuith-Raing. South of the Quiraing is The Old Man of

Storr, a bare mountain that resembles the face of an old man.

The MacLeods and MacDonalds were the two most powerful clans after the Norse period. Dunvegan Castle has been occupied by the MacLeods since it was built in the 13th century. Armadale Castle, Knock Castle, and Dunscaith Castle are ruined buildings that belonged to the MacDonalds.

Dunscaith Castle

Dunscaith was built on a rock bluff overlooking the ocean. It is believed to be the home of Scáthach, a woman warrior of Irish myth. Dunscaith traded hands between the MacLeods and the MacDonalds in the 14th and 15th centuries. The MacDonalds abandoned it in the 17th century.

Skye is home to two whisky distilleries, Talisker and Torabhaig. Talisker was opened in 1831 and is the oldest distillery on Skye. Two separate fires caused major damage in the 20th century. Talisker was a favorite of Robert Louis Stevenson who wrote, "The king o' drinks, as I conceive it, Talisker, Isla, or Glenlivet!"[iii]

Islay and Jura

The third largest isle of the Inner Hebrides was also the center of an island empire. Islay, pronounced "eye-la," was the home of the semi-independent MacDonald clan. Somerled built a fortress here in the 12th century. His heirs built Finlaggan Castle in the 13th century. They ruled until 1493 when King James IV of Scotland removed them from power for supporting the English King. James ordered Finlaggan Castle be demolished to subdue the ambition of the MacDonald heirs.

Islay was passed to the Campbells of Shawfield. David Campbell was responsible for the development of Bowmore, the first planned village in Scotland. The town was built on a grid pattern with wide streets. The Kilarrow church is unique for its round design. Bowmore is the largest town on Islay with a population of 700.

Whisky is a major source of jobs on Islay. Nine distilleries call it home. They are: Ardbeg, Bowmore, Bunnahabhain,

Caol Ila, Kilchoman, Lagavulin, Laphroaig, Ardnahoe, and Bruichladdich. Water and barley are key ingredients of whisky, and they are available on Islay in abundance. Islay soil is fertile with a high concentration of peat.

Islay and Jura are separated by the narrow Sound of Islay. Access between the islands is provided by a ten-minute ferry ride. The rugged island of Jura is home to only 200 people, compared to Islay's population of 3,000. The skyline is dominated by the Paps of Jura, three breast-shaped quartzite mountains. The tallest, Beinn an Óir rises to 2,575 feet.

Red deer outnumber people on Jura by twenty-five to one. The herd is reported to contain 5,000 animals. Private estates on Jura provide deer stalking services for hunters. There is one distillery on Jura, the Jura Distillery.

The novelist George Orwell lived on Jura when he wrote *Nineteen Eighty-Four*. He nearly lost his life when a boat he was piloting overturned in the dangerous Gulf of Corryvreckan. This part of the ocean is especially treacherous and contains whirlpools.

Iona and Mull

The small island of Iona is known as an important religious center. St. Columba established a monastery on Iona in the sixth century. Iona became a center from which Christianity flowed to the Picts and the Scots. Viking raids in the ninth century prompted the majority of monks to relocate to Ireland.

A stone church was built on the site of the original abbey in the 13th century. A nunnery was established south of the church. The center ceased to be used after the Scottish Reformation and was dismantled. The abbey church was rebuilt in the 20th century.

The abbey cemetery contains the remains of several dozen Scottish, Norwegian, and Irish kings. Among them is the Red King, known as MacBeth. None of the graves can be identified today as the writing on the monuments has worn away.

Iona lies less than a mile west of Mull. A ferry transports visitors to Iona from the Fionnphort Ferry Terminal. The abbey is located about 3/8 mile from the ferry landing. Several operators provide tours that include Mull and Iona.

Mull is the second largest island of the Inner Hebrides. The Tobermory distillery is located on Mull. The skyline is dominated by Ben More which rises to 3,169 feet. Mull is home to two MacLean castles, Duart and Moy. Duart Castle was built in the 13th century. It was demolished by Clan Campbell, under order of the Scottish Privy Council, in the late 17th century. Clan MacLean bought the property in the 20th century and restored the castle. Moy Castle was built in the 14th century and is an abandoned ruin.

Outer Hebrides

As the name suggests, the Outer Hebrides are farther away from the Scottish mainland than the Inner Hebrides. This island group is comprised of sixty-five islands, only fifteen of which are inhabited. Total population of the Outer Hebrides is 26,000.

Lewis and Harris is the largest island in Scotland. It is also the most populous with 21,000 people. Lewis and Harris is a single island composed of two parts. The northern two-thirds of the island is called Lewis, while the southern one-third is Harris. The parts are often referred as separate islands even though they belong to the same land mass. Stornoway is the largest town with a population of 4,600.

The Callanish Stones is a stone circle that was built around 3,000 BC. It is located west of Stornoway on Lewis. The circle consists of thirteen stones that are about nine feet high. There are several prehistoric sites in the immediate area. Lewis and Harris was dominated by Clan MacLeod after the Viking period.

Harris tweed fabric is a major industry. It is a handwoven wool cloth that is produced in the homes of islanders. According to an Act of the British Parliament, the fabric must be produced entirely in the Outer Hebrides in order to use the name "Harris Tweed."

Fife

The peninsula of Fife lies to the north of Edinburgh and is bounded by the Firth of Forth and the Firth of Tay. The area has a population of 367,000. Fishing villages dot the eastern coast along the North Sea. Scottish kings lived in Fife and one queen was imprisoned here. An American country music icon performed in Fife.

St. Andrews

Named after the Apostle Andrew, St. Andrews was the religious center of medieval Scotland. The massive ruin of St. Andrews Cathedral is located on the east side of town overlooking the North Sea.

St. Andrews Cathedral

The cathedral was the largest building in Scotland when it was built in the 14th century. King Robert the Bruce was in attendance when the cathedral was consecrated. The building fell into disrepair during the Scottish Reformation.

St. Andrews Castle is a short walk from the cathedral. It was home to the bishops of the church. It was attacked and damaged during the Wars of Scottish Independence. The castle was allowed to decay after the Scottish Reformation.

The University of St. Andrews is the third oldest university in Great Britain, behind Oxford and Cambridge. It was founded in the early 15th century. Famous alumni include William and Kate, the Prince and Princess of Wales. The American author James Michener attended St. Andrews.

One of the most famous golf courses in the world is the Old Course at St. Andrews. The Royal and Ancient Golf Club of St. Andrews was organized in 1754. It is one of the oldest golf clubs in the world. The Open, or British Open, is held at the St. Andrews Old Course every five years.

The Old Course is closed on Sundays. Visitors are allowed to walk the course on that day and take pictures at the famous Swilcan Bridge on the 18th fairway.

The Royal and Ancient Golf Club of St. Andrews and the 18th green of the Old Course

Visitors to St. Andrews can walk to all the destinations in a few hours: cathedral, castle, university, and the Old Course. They are located near each other and there are no steep hills to navigate. St. Andrews has several eating establishments and tourist shops.

Dunfermline

The largest town in Fife became the home of Scottish kings when Malcolm III moved to Dunfermline in the 11th century. Malcolm's wife, Queen Margaret, established a new church near Malcolm's Tower. The church evolved into Dunfermline Abbey. It is the burial site for many members of Scottish royalty, including Robert the Bruce.

The abbey was destroyed during the Scottish Reformation in the 16th century.

Dunfermline was used as a royal residence from the time of Malcolm III to the Union of the Crowns in the 15th century. Dunfermline Palace is located adjacent to the abbey. It is unclear when the palace was built or converted to a royal residence. It was abandoned in the 17th century and fell into disrepair.

American industrialist Andrew Carnegie was born in Dunfermline in 1848. He became one of the richest individuals in history. He chose to become a philanthropist later in his life and gave away most of his fortune.

Dunfermline is about ten miles northeast of Edinburgh. It is a short train ride from Edinburgh Waverly station.

St. Monans

The pretty church in the small fishing village of St. Monans sits next to the sea shore. It is one of the oldest churches in Scotland that is still in use. The date of original construction on the site of St. Monans Old Kirk is debatable. The church was most likely built in the 14th century by King David I. It was rebuilt to its present state in the 19th century.

American country music superstar Johnny Cash recorded part of his 1981 Christmas Special inside the St. Monans Old Kirk. Cash sang traditional Christmas carols with local school children. The "Man In Black" had family roots in the Fife area and made several trips to Scotland to visit and perform.

St. Monans Old Kirk

Anstruther

Of all the fishing villages along the Fife coast, I think Anstruther may be the prettiest. It is also the largest. The harbor is protected from the sea by a wall. Boats rest on the bottom of the harbor during low tide and float when the tide comes in. Boaters must pay attention to the tide schedule in order to avoid being stranded at sea.

Anstruther is home to a relic of the Cold War. A secret bunker was built in the 1950's to be a nuclear command center in the event of a nuclear attack. The bunker is no longer a secret and is a tourist attraction. It can be visited from February through November. You can learn more at secretbunker.co.uk.

Falkland

A hunting lodge was built at Falkland in the 12th century. It was enlarged over the years and became a country castle of the later Stuart monarchs. Falkland Palace functioned as a retreat from the politics of Edinburgh. It featured a tennis court, gardens, and hunting grounds. Deer and boar were contained within the grounds for purposes of hunting by the royals.

King James V died at Falkland Palace in December 1542 at the age of 30. His only legitimate heir, Mary Queen of Scots, was only six days old when he died. Mary, a Catholic, ascended to the Scottish throne at the height of the Scottish reformation. She would butt heads with the reformer John Knox. Mary made several visits to Falkland during her reign. She played tennis on the court that exists to this day.

Mary's ill-fated marriage to Lord Bothwell contributed to her downfall. Scottish nobility turned against her and she was forced to abdicate the throne in 1567. Mary was imprisoned at Lochleven Castle, about twelve miles southwest of Falkland. She eventually fled to England where she was imprisoned at Carlisle Castle by the

English. Mary was beheaded in 1587 after being convicted of conspiracy against Queen Elizabeth I.

Falkland Palace

Falkland is twenty-four miles northeast of Dunfermline by car, and thirty-five miles north of Edinburgh. It is a small village of 1,100 people with shops, restaurants, and hotels.

Glasgow

The largest city in Scotland is overlooked by many tourists. Glasgow is a city of museums and an important hub for air and train travel. There are many guided tours that depart from Glasgow. It may be the most American-looking city in Scotland. The city is laid out on a grid system. The architecture is dominated by the Victorian style, similar to many east coast American cities.

Glasgow was transformed during the Industrial Revolution. It became one of the most important shipbuilding cities in the world during the 19th century. There were six major shipbuilders based along the River Clyde at one time. The shipbuilding industry declined after World War II. China now builds more ships than any other nation.

HMY Britannia was built in Glasgow in 1953. Other famous ships built in Glasgow include RMS Queen Mary, RMS Lusitania, and Cutty Sark. A tall sailing ship, the Glenlee, is moored outside the Riverside Museum of Transport and Travel, one of the top-rated attractions in Glasgow. The museum is situated on the riverbank of the Clyde. It contains displays on the history of shipbuilding and other modes of transport, including trains and autos.

The massive Kelvingrove Art Gallery and Museum is located in downtown Glasgow a short walk from the Riverside Museum. The museum includes works by

Rembrandt, Gauguin, Renoir, Monet, and Dali. It is one of the most visited attractions in Glasgow and it is free.

The Clydeside Distillery is also within walking distance from the Riverside Museum. Tours are available. Their whisky is made from water sourced from Loch Katrine. The distillery is open seven days a week and includes a gift shop and café.

Glasgow is the center of Scottish football (soccer). Scottish professional football has been dominated by two teams from the Glasgow area: Rangers and Celtic. Their stadiums are only five miles apart. Rangers Football Club has won more Scottish Premier Championships than any other team. Their home, Ibrox Stadium, is open for guided tours. The cost of a tour for a family of four is £35. Celtic Park is also open for tours. Hampden Park Stadium is home to the Scottish National Football Team.

Glasgow has achieved notoriety in recent years for massive building murals. There are over two dozen large murals painted on the sides of buildings in the downtown area. Plan on walking for three to four hours if you want to see all of them.

ENTERTAINMENT FRANCHISES

Scotland is known for its stunning scenery and historic sites. Many of these locations have been featured in film and television. This section of the book provides information on major entertainment franchises that have been filmed in Scotland.

Outlander

The popular series is based on the books of Diana Gabaldon. The opening credits and many outdoor scenes are filmed in Glencoe. Cairngorms National Park is also used for its stunning landscapes.

Claire Randall travels through time to 18th century Scotland through the stones of Craig Na Dun. This location is fictional. The stones do represent the alleged mystical properties of numerous ancient stone circles that are scattered throughout Scotland.

The village of Falkland is used to represent 1940s Inverness is Season One. The ghost of Jamie Fraser sees Claire from the fountain. Sam Heughan, who plays the part of Jamie, is a native of Scotland. The village of Culross is featured as the town of Cranesmuir.

Two locations in the village of Doune are used in the series. Doune Castle represents Castle Leoch, the fictional home of Clan MacKenzie. Deanston Distillery serves as Jamie's cousin's wine warehouse in Le Harve.

Three Outlander filming locations are located in close proximity to the west of Edinburgh. Blackness Castle is used as the filming location for Fort William, where Jamie is imprisoned by Jack Randall. Midhope Castle is filmed as Lallybroch, the home of Jamie Fraser. Linlithgow Palace stands in for Wentworth Prison.

The Battle of Culloden was not filmed at the actual battlefield since it is a historical monument and grave site. It was filmed northeast of Glasgow at Cumbernauld Glen. Jamie fought for the Jacobite cause. Knowing the Jacobites would be slaughtered and he would probably die, Jamie sent Claire back through the stones at Craig Na Dun. Jamie survived the battle and its aftermath. Claire would eventually return to the 18th century and find Jamie.

Outlander guided tours range from one-day to eight-days in length. Several operators provide these tours that cater to the fans of the show.

Falkland Fountain

Dunlanrig Castle, in the Galloway region, was used as the estate of the Duke of Sandringham in Season 2. Jamie Fraser and his compatriots captured the Duke and relieved him of his head. The large castle was built in the 17th century of red sandstone. It is called The Pink Castle because of its distinct color.

Dunlanrig was home to Clan Douglas. It is located about forty miles south of Glasgow. Tours and lodging can be booked at drumlanrigcastle.co.uk. The castle grounds include a café, Victorian gardens, and a gift shop.

Game of Thrones

The only filming site for Game of Thrones in Scotland is Doune Castle. It was used in the pilot episode as Winterfell.

Harry Potter

J.K. Rowling wrote the first Harry Potter novel while living in Edinburgh. She did much of her writing at The Elephant House cafe. George Heriot's School, which is visible from The Elephant House, is believed to be the inspiration for Hogwarts.

Glenfinnan Viaduct in the Highlands is featured in several films as the train makes its way to Hogwarts (see page 46). Limited Harry Potter seating is available on the Jacobite Steam Train in first class.

Glencoe valley was used for scenes in the films, most notably Hagrid's Hut and Quidditch matches. Loch Shiel was filmed as the Black Lake, or Great Lake, at Hogwarts. This beautiful fresh-water loch is located near the Glenfinnan Viaduct. Doune Castle was used as the main filming location for Hogwarts in "Harry Potter and the Sorcerer's Stone."

The Hogwarts Express: LMS Class 5MT locomotive

Visitors to Edinburgh can book one of several Harry Potter walking tours. They typically last two hours.

James Bond

Bond, James Bond. The British agent, code name 007, has been portrayed in twenty-five official Bond movies over the past sixty plus years. Visitors to London can book Bond walking tours to visit filming locations in the city. The film franchise has many ties to Scotland; the fictional Bond was Scottish.

Ian Fleming, the writer of the original James Bond spy novels, served in British Naval Intelligence during World War II. His work provided a fertile field of knowledge for his literary career. Fleming wrote the first Bond novel, *Casino Royale*, in 1952. The popularity of Fleming's books evolved into film. The first Bond movie, *Dr. No*, was released in 1962.

Fleming was born to a wealthy English family. His father, Valentine Fleming, built a house at Arnisdale in a remote area in the Highlands. Valentine was killed during World War I in 1917, just one year after Arnisdale House was completed. Ian would spend time at Arnisdale during his youth. Arnisdale can only be accessed by automobile. It is located on a single-track road south of Glenelg on the mainland near Skye.

Duntrune Castle was used for the exterior scenes of the MI6 Scottish Headquarters in *From Russia with Love*. This former Campbell residence has been in the hands of the Malcolm family since the 18th century. Duntrune is fifty miles west of Glasgow on the Kintyre Peninsula. Cottages on the estate are available for tourist lodging (duntrunecastle.com). Duntrune is a private estate and tours are offered on a limited basis. Please visit their website to inquire.

Eilean Donan Castle served as the Scottish operations center for MI6 in *The World Is Not Enough*. The Glencoe area was used as a backdrop during the final scenes of *Skyfall*. Bond's ancestral home, Skyfall Lodge, is fictional. The location is real. The driving scene featuring Bond's vintage Aston Martin DB5 was filmed on the A82 road.

Monty Python

Doune Castle was the filming location for several scenes in *Monty Python and the Holy Grail* including Lancelot's attack, the French taunters, the Trojan Rabbit, and interior shots. The 1975 film was a parody of King Arthur's quest to find the Holy Grail. The low-budget movie achieved commercial success in the United Kingdom and North America.

Castle Stalker was used for Castle Aaarrrggghhh in *Monty Python and the Holy* Grail. The island tower house is privately owned and is open for limited tours (castlestalker.com). It is located twenty-five miles north of Oban. The land on which Castle Stalker sits has been held by the MacDougalls, Stewarts, and Campbells. Castle Stalker was purchased by D. R. Stewart Allward in 1965 and refurbished.

Braveheart

The 1995 film depicted the life of William Wallace, who led the Scots in the First War of Scottish Independence. *Braveheart*, starring Mel Gibson, was a commercial success and increased the awareness of Scotland around the world. The movie contains numerous historical errors. A Scottish tour guide once told me there are over forty errors in the movie, but most Scots have shrugged it off because of the business the movie brought to their homeland.

Glen Nevis was the filming site for many of the outdoor scenes in *Braveheart*. Doune Castle was used for some of the interior scenes. Edinburgh was used for its historical architecture.

William Wallace became the driving force of Scottish resistance against the English and defeated them in 1297 at the Battle of Stirling Bridge. The movie accurately portrays that Wallace captured the support of his countrymen due to his leadership skills. He is considered a national hero to this day.

The most glaring error in the movie is the lack of a bridge in the Battle of Stirling Bridge. The movie depicts the battle in an open field. The Scots were not equipped for open warfare and relied on guerilla tactics. The Scots attacked the English while they were in the process of crossing the bridge over the river Forth. English knights were shoved into the boggy ground where their horses and heavy armor when ineffective. The wooden bridge collapsed during the battle. A stone bridge was built on the site sometime around 1500.

Stirling Old Bridge: built on the site of the Battle of Stirling Bridge

The romantic relationship portrayed in the movie between Wallace and the English princess Isabella is fictional. Isabella was under ten years old at the time of the events in the movie and was living in France. The Scots were shown wearing face paint during battle. This is unlikely. Their pagan ancestors, the Picts, may have used face paint. The Scots were Catholic and would not have carried on this tradition.

There has been much debate about the clothing worn by the Scots in *Braveheart*. The traditional kilt, as depicted in the movie had not been invented yet. The Scots warriors likely wore clothing that resembled a tunic. The modern kilt was invented sometime during the 18th century. Clan tartans, with unique patterns for each clan, were created in the 19th century.

Chariots of Fire

The opening scene of the 1981 movie was filmed at West Sands in St. Andrews. The Carlton Hotel in the opening is actually the clubhouse of the Royal and Ancient Golf Club.

West Sands Beach

Chariots of Fire won Academy Awards for Best Picture, Best Original Screenplay, and Best Original Score. The story follows runners Harold Abraham and Eric Liddell as they represented Great Britain at the 1924 Olympics in Paris.

The theme music of *Chariots of Fire* was played by the London Symphony Orchestra at the opening ceremony of the 2012 London Olympics. Rowan Atkinson was featured on keyboard. Several scenes from the movie were filmed in Edinburgh.

THE WATER OF LIFE

O thou, my muse! Guid, auld Scotch drink!
Whether thro' wimplin worms thou jink,
Or, richly brown, ream owre the brink,
In glorious feam,
Inspire me, till I lisp an' wink,
To sing thy name![iv]   Robert Burns

The popularity of whisky is deeply rooted in Scotland's history, culture, and natural resources. There is much debate about who invented whisky, the Scots or the Irish. Distillation techniques were likely invented in the birthplace of civilization and arrived in the region through Middle Eastern and Mediterranean trade routes. A common theory is that the methods of distillation were brought to Scotland by traveling monks.

The origins of the word "whisky" gives credence to the claim that Ireland and Scotland are the birthplace of the drink as we know it. Whisky is an anglicization of the Gaelic word *uisge*, pronounced "ooshkih." Whisky is called *aqua vitae*, or "water of life" in Latin. The Gaelic translation is *uisge beatha*, pronounced "ooshkih beh-ha."

Whisky is a major export of Scotland. Many of the distilleries in Scotland are owned by multinational corporations like Diageo. A few are still privately owned. Multi-day guided tours are available for whisky pilgrims who want to learn more about Scotland's popular export. Islay is a popular destination of these tours because of the number of distilleries in the area and the stark beauty of the island. Travelers can also book tours through the website of most distilleries.

The natural resources required for whisky production are abundant in Scotland: water, barley, and peat. Pure water, available from natural sources, is essential for the production process. Peat fires used to dry the malted barley add a smoky flavor. The cool temperate climate influences the aging process and contributes to the flavor associated with good whisky.

Talisker Distillery, Isle of Skye

Regional variations of whisky have evolved. The whiskeys of Islay, for example, are known for their peated and smoky flavor. Speyside whiskies are lighter and fruity. The differences in shapes and sizes of whisky stills also contributes to the unique properties of whisky from each distillery.

Bourbon is similar to whisky but there are distinct differences. Bourbon is specific to the United States. By law, bourbon mash must contain 51% corn. Whisky grains may contain a mixture of barley, wheat, corn, and rye. Bourbon must be aged in new charred oak barrels. Whisky is typically aged in wooden barrels that were once used to age bourbon or sherry.

Like many industries, whisky has gone through cycles of boom and bust. Whisky production requires a lot of energy. The cost of energy could be a challenge for the industry in coming years. The United Kingdom is not energy-independent and costs have increased dramatically.

Two new distilleries have been built near population centers. This will make it easier for visitors to experience whisky production first-hand. Port of Leith distillery, near Edinburgh, is distilling gin until their single malt whisky is available. The distillery is a short walk from HMS Britannia. A bar is located on the top floor with views of the city. Uilebheist Distillery in Inverness opened in 2023. They are brewing several styles of beer, in addition to producing whisky. Uilebheist is Scots Gaelic for "monster." Nessie would approve. The distillery is located on the east bank of the River Ness, a short walk from downtown.

Visitors with limited time can visit The Scotch Whisky Experience located at 354 Castlehill at the top of the Royal Mile in Edinburgh. It is a short walk from Edinburgh Castle. The Silver Tour currently costs £23 and lasts about an hour. The tour includes the story of whisky and describes the process of production. Visitors learn about the different regions of Scotland whisky. A dram of single malt whisky is included. Visit scotchwhiskyexperience.com for more information.

THE NAMELESS CLAN

While there's leaves in the forest and foam on the river,
MacGregor despite them, shall flourish forever![v]
                                        Sir Walter Scott

Clan Gregor (MacGregor) occupied the lands of Glenorchy, Glenstrae, and Glengyle in the southern Highlands. Much evidence has been presented to tie the lineage of Clan Gregor to ancient royalty, including Kenneth MacAlpin and Gregor MacDungal. I will leave that assessment to those with more knowledge of ancient Highland history. For those who want to dig deeper into this mystery, I suggest the book *Clan Gregor* by Forbes MacGregor. My head was spinning after a few hours of reading the twists, turns, and tangents of events from the late Pictish era.

Most historians identify Cham MacGregor as the first known chief of Clan Gregor in the late 14th century. By this time, Clan Campbell was expanding to the east. Neil Campbell had fought for Robert the Bruce at Bannockburn in 1314. He had married Bruce's sister, Mary. The Bruce granted lordship over the lands around Loch Awe to the Campbells in return for their support. The MacGregors were effectively vassals of the Campbells at this point.

A tenuous coexistence between the MacGregors and the expansionist Campbells would remain in place for the next three hundred years. A feud erupted in the middle 16th century when Grey Colin Campbell imposed stricter terms of existence upon the MacGregors. The MacGregors rebelled against these terms. This episode ended with Grey Colin executing the MacGregor chief in 1570.

The MacGregors angered the king when they murdered his forester, John Drummond, in 1589. Drummond had hanged some of the clan for poaching deer. The Battle of Glen Fruin between the MacGregors and the Colquhouns in 1603 would raise the king's ire to a breaking point. The MacGregors routed Clan Colquhoun even though they were outnumbered two to one. Colquhoun casualties numbered between 150 and 200.

King James VI and his Privy Council enacted acts of proscription upon the MacGregors in February and April 1603. The acts called for the MacGregors to be prosecuted, hunted, followed, and pursued with fire and sword. The name MacGregor, or Gregor, was abolished and its leaders were to be eliminated. Clan members were called upon to renounce their name and take another. Clan chief Alasdair MacGregor and several of his kin were hung in Edinburgh adjacent to St. Giles Cathedral in 1604. The clan withdrew deeper into the glens with their main base in Glengyle. The proscription of the MacGregors would not be lifted until 1774.

There are three possible sources of blame for the battle at Glen Fruin: MacGregor, Colquhoun, or Campbell. The MacGregors had lifted (stolen) cattle by the hundreds and the Colquhouns had enough of it. The MacGregors sought retribution on the Colquhouns for hanging two MacGregors who slaughtered a sheep for food. The Earl of Argyll (Campbell) was supposedly in a position of authority over the MacGregors. Did he encourage the MacGregors to attack the Colquhouns so he could expand into their land? The real reason for Glen Fruin is difficult for us to say at this juncture in time. I think we can easily say, "It's complicated."

The most famous MacGregor, Rob Roy, was immortalized in the Walter Scott novel. He was born in Glengyle on the banks of Loch Katrine in 1671. He used his mother's maiden name of Campbell when convenient because MacGregor was outlawed. Rob participated in the Jacobite uprisings of 1689 and 1715. He was a farmer and cattle dealer. Rob formed the Highland Watch which provided protection against theft for those who paid him protection money. Many historians claim this was the stimulus for the word "blackmail."

A financial dispute between Rob and the Duke of Montrose led to a feud. Rob was declared an outlaw and his house at Inversnaid was burned. MacGregor responded by lifting cattle from Montrose and stealing rents. He would be imprisoned in 1722 and pardoned in 1727. Rob moved to the Balquidder area at the end of his life. He died in his home in 1734 and is buried at Balquidder Kirk. Rob is portrayed by Liam Neeson in the 1995 film *Rob Roy*.

Stronachlachar Pier, Loch Katrine

Research indicates that my ancestor who immigrated to America from Scotland changed his name from MacGregor sometime around 1652. The trail gets cold and murky at that point. The name of MacGregor was outlawed. Ministers in Scotland were banned from baptizing or christening any child with the name MacGregor by King Charles I in 1633.

Recommended sites for MacGregor descendants to visit in Scotland:

- Loch Katrine
- Balquidder Kirk
- St. Giles Cathedral - Edinburgh

THE CAMPBELLS ARE COMING

One of the largest and most successful of the clans, the Campbells were adept at politics and strategy. They were shrewd in backing the winning side in major conflicts. They backed Robert the Bruce in the Wars of Scottish Independence. The main Campbell group, Argyll, backed the English Crown in the Jacobite uprisings. The Campbells were of Briton ancestry and intermarried with other Highland groups.

The first known use of the name was Dugald of Lochawe. He was called Cambeul. Many believe this is because he tended to talk out of one side of his mouth. Cam Beul in Gaelic means "wry mouth" or "crooked mouth." The family began to use the name Cambel in the 13th century.

A major turning point for the clan occurred when Robert the Bruce granted them official charters for the land around Loch Awe. The Campbells had supported Bruce at his lowest point during his struggle with King Edward I. They would expand throughout the southwest Highlands, down the Kintyre peninsula, and into the Inner Hebrides.

Colin Campbell, 1st Earl of Argyll, expanded the reach of the clan into central Scotland. He received Castle Gloom through marriage to Isabel Stewart. It was renamed Castle Campbell in 1490. Archibald, the 4th Earl, converted to Presbyterianism in the 16th century. The reformer John

Knox visited Castle Campbell on two occasions. Mary Queen of Scots visited Castle Campbell in 1653 to attend the wedding of her relative James Stewart to Margaret, sister of the 5th Earl.

Campbell support for the Scottish monarchy continued to provide benefits. Archibald Campbell, the 7th Earl, was granted the Kintyre peninsula in 1607. These lands had been held by the MacDonalds. The Campbells of Cawdor were allowed to purchase Islay in 1615. Islay was developed by the Campbells. Walter Frederick Campbell was forced to sell Islay in 1853 because he had been driven bankrupt by the potato blight.

Archibald Campbell, 9th Earl of Argyll, purchased a home near Stirling Castle in 1666. Argyll's Lodging would provide the Campbells a residence within walking distance of Stirling Castle. It would remain in the family for almost a hundred years. The English Duke of Cumberland, son of King George II and leader of the government army, stayed at Argyll's Lodging during the last Jacobite uprising.

Argyll's Lodging

The Argyll Campbells supported the English Crown with resources during the Jacobite uprisings. The 5th Duke of Argyll led government forces and served under the Duke of Cumberland at Culloden in 1746. It is said the government forces under Campbell marched with bagpipes to the tune "The Campbells are Coming." A small number of Campbells fought on the Jacobite side at Culloden. Campbell of Ardslignish fell while leading Jacobite soldiers. Culloden has a similarity to the American Civil War in that families fought on both sides.

Recommended sites for Campbell descendants to visit in Scotland:

- Inverary Castle – home to the current Duke of Argyll
- Castle Campbell
- Argyll's Lodging - Stirling
- Kilchurn Castle – ruined castle that was home to the Glenorchy Campbells. Kilchurn is under the care of Historic Environment Scotland. Their website indicates the castle is closed for conservation works. Travelers can view the exterior from the A85 and A819 roads along the northeast shore of Loch Awe.

Clan Campbell became large and successful. There are almost twenty castles associated with the clan.

TOP TEN CASTLES

With approximately one thousand castles in Scotland, the decision on which ones to visit can be daunting. I have listed my top ten castles in this chapter. This list is completely arbitrary and based on my own preferences which I'll describe for the reader. I expect this list will change as I visit more castles.

1. Stirling Castle
2. Edinburgh Castle
3. Palace of Holyroodhouse
4. Eilean Donan Castle
5. Inverary Castle
6. Castle Campbell
7. Falkland Palace
8. Linlithgow Palace
9. Doune Castle
10. St. Andrews Castle

Stirling and Edinburgh Castles top the list. Both of these imposing structures dominate the skyline in their respective cities. Both have a long history tied to the nation of Scotland. Stirling was home to the Stuart monarchs. The Honours of Scotland and the Stone of Destiny are housed at Edinburgh Castle.

The Palace of Holyroodhouse is important because it is the official home of the British monarch in Scotland. It is located just a mile from Edinburgh Castle.

Eilean Donan Castle is one of the most beautiful spots in the country. It has been used as a filming location in several films.

Inverary Castle and Castle Campbell are important locations for Clan Campbell. Both locations have been visited by Scottish royalty.

St. Andrews Castle

Falkland Palace was a hunting retreat for the Stuart Monarchs. The village of Falkland has been used as a filming location for *Outlander*.

Linlithgow Palace was the birthplace of two Scottish monarchs. King Edward I of England visited twice during his efforts to assert his superiority.

Doune Castle may be the most filmed location in all of Scotland.

St. Andrews Castle was the home of the leaders of the medieval Catholic church in Scotland. It sits on a bluff overlooking the North Sea.

ABOUT THE AUTHOR

Richard McGee is a business professional and historian with Scottish ancestry. He has operations experience in the healthcare, manufacturing, and mining industries. Richard's company, Glenstrae LLC, was founded in 2023. The company produces print and digital content on the topics of leadership and history. His first book, *Five Star Culture*, was published in 2023.

Richard, and his wife Joyce have ancestral connections to Scotland. Richard has ties to Clan MacGregor, while Joyce has ties to Clan Campbell.

Readers may visit www.richard-mcgee.com or www.amazon.com/author/remcgee for more information about Richard and Glenstrae LLC.

RECOMMENDED READING

Rick Steves Scotland by Rick Steves with Cameron Hewitt

Essential Scotland by Fodor's

The Highland Clans by Alistair Moffat

Clan Gregor by Forbes MacGregor

Inverary Castle and Garden by The Duchess of Argyll

Selected Poems by Robert Burns

The Campbells by John MacKay

The Clanlands Almanac by Sam Heughan and Graham McTavish

ENDNOTES

[i] Topbanana. "File:Scotland Map.png" Wikipedia Commons. 2023. https://commons.wikimedia.org/wiki/File:Scotland_Map.png

[ii] Burns, R. *Complete Poems and Songs of Robert Burns*, Waverly Books, 2012

[iii] Stevenson, R. *The Collected Poems of Robert Louis Stevenson*, Edinburgh University Press, 2003.

[iv] Burns, R. *Selected Poetry,* Penguin Books, 1991.

[v] Scott, W. *The Poetical Works of Sir Walter Scott*, Ticknor & Company, 1887.

Made in the USA
Las Vegas, NV
10 December 2024

13830657R00066